Second Corinthians

STUDY GUIDE

Jerome Kodell, O.S.B.

LITTLE ROCK SCRIPTURE STUDY
Little Rock, Arkansas

THE LITURGICAL PRESS
Collegeville, Minnesota

Office of the Bishop

DIOCESE OF LITTLE ROCK

2500 North Tyler Street • P.O. Box 7239 • Little Rock, Arkansas 72217 • (501) 664-0340 • Fax (501) 664-6304

Dear Friends in Christ,

The Bible comes to us as both a gift and an opportunity. It is a gift of God who loves us enough to communicate with us. The only way to enjoy the gift is to open and savor it. The Bible is also an opportunity to actually meet God who is present in the stories, teachings, people, and prayers that fill its pages.

I encourage you to open your Bibles in anticipation that God will do something good in your life. I encourage you to take advantage of the opportunity to meet God in prayer, study, and small-group discussion.

Little Rock Scripture Study offers materials that are simple to use, and a method that has been tested by time. The questions in this study guide will direct your study, help you to understand the passages you are reading, and challenge you to relate the Scriptures to your own life experiences.

Allow the Word of God to form you as a disciple of the Lord Jesus. Accept the challenge to be "transformed by the renewal of your mind" (Romans 12:2). Above all, receive God's Word as his gift, and act upon it.

Sincerely in Christ,

✢ J. Peter Sartain
Bishop of Little Rock

Sacred Scripture

"The Church has always venerated the divine Scriptures just as she venerates the body of the Lord, since from the table of both the word of God and of the body of Christ she unceasingly receives and offers to the faithful the bread of life, especially in the sacred liturgy. She has always regarded the Scriptures together with sacred tradition as the supreme rule of faith, and will ever do so. For, inspired by God and committed once and for all to writing, they impart the word of God himself without change, and make the voice of the Holy Spirit resound in the words of the prophets and apostles. Therefore, like the Christian religion itself, all the preaching of the Church must be nourished and ruled by sacred Scripture. For in the sacred books, the Father who is in heaven meets His children with great love and speaks with them; and the force and power in the word of God is so great that it remains the support and energy of the Church, the strength of faith for her sons, the food of the soul, the pure and perennial source of spiritual life."
Vatican II, Dogmatic Constitution on Divine Revelation, no. 21.

INTERPRETATION OF SACRED SCRIPTURE

"Since God speaks in sacred Scripture through men in human fashion, the interpreter of sacred Scripture, in order to see clearly what God wanted to communicate to us, should carefully investigate what meaning the sacred writers really intended, and what God wanted to manifest by means of their words.

"Those who search out the intention of the sacred writers must, among other things, have regard for 'literary forms.' For truth is proposed and expressed in a variety of ways, depending on whether a text is history of one kind or another, or whether its form is that of prophecy, poetry, or some other type of speech. The interpreter must investigate what meaning the sacred writer intended to express and actually expressed in particular circumstances as he used contemporary literary forms in accordance with the situation of his own time and culture. For the correct understanding of what the sacred author wanted to assert, due attention must be paid to the customary and characteristic styles of perceiving, speaking, and narrating which prevailed at the time of the sacred writer, and to the customs men normally followed in that period in their everyday dealings with one another."

Vatican II, Dogmatic Constitution on Divine Revelation, no. 12.

Instructions

MATERIALS FOR THE STUDY

This Study Guide: Second Corinthians

Bible: The New American Bible with Revised New Testament or The New Jerusalem Bible is recommended. Paraphrased editions are discouraged as they offer little if any help when facing difficult textual questions. Choose a Bible you feel free to write in or underline.

Commentary: The Collegeville Bible Commentary: New Testament Series, Volume 7, *First Corinthians, Second Corinthians*, by Mary Ann Getty (The Liturgical Press) is used with this study. The assigned pages are found at the beginning of each lesson.

ADDITIONAL MATERIALS

Bible Dictionary: *The Dictionary of the Bible* by John L. McKenzie (Simon & Schuster) is highly recommended as an additional reference.

Notebook: A notebook may be used for lecture notes and your personal reflections.

WEEKLY LESSONS

Lesson 1—2 Cor 1–2
Lesson 2—2 Cor 3–4
Lesson 3—2 Cor 5–7
Lesson 4—2 Cor 8–9

Lesson 5—2 Cor 10–11
Lesson 6—2 Cor 12–13

YOUR DAILY PERSONAL STUDY

The first step is prayer. Open your heart and mind to God. Reading Scripture is an opportunity to listen to God who loves you. Pray that the same Holy Spirit who guided the formation of Scripture will inspire you to correctly understand what you read and empower you to make what you read a part of your life.

The next step is commitment. Daily spiritual food is as necessary as food for the body. This study is divided into daily units. Schedule a regular time and place for your study, as free from distractions as possible. Allow about twenty minutes a day. Make it a daily appointment with God.

As you begin each lesson read the assigned chapters of Scripture found at the beginning of each lesson, the footnotes in your Bible, and then the indicated pages of the commentary. This preparation will give you an overview of the entire lesson and help you to appreciate the context of individual passages.

As you reflect on Scripture, ask yourself these four questions:

1. *What does the Scripture passage say?*
   Read the passage slowly and reflectively. Use your imagination to picture the scene or enter into it.

2. *What does the Scripture passage mean?*
   Read the footnotes and the commentary to help you understand what the sacred writers intended and what God wanted to communicate by means of their words.

3. *What does the Scripture passage mean to me?*
   Meditate on the passage. God's Word is living and powerful. What is God saying to you today? How does the Scripture passage apply to your life today?

4. *What am I going to do about it?*
   Try to discover how God may be challenging you in this

passage. An encounter with God contains a challenge to know God's will and follow it more closely in daily life.

THE QUESTIONS ASSIGNED FOR EACH DAY

Read the questions and references for each day. The questions are designed to help you listen to God's Word and to prepare you for the weekly small-group discussion.

Some of the questions can be answered briefly and objectively by referring to the Bible references and the commentary *(What does the passage say?)*. Some will lead you to a better understanding of how the Scriptures apply to the Church, sacraments, and society *(What does the passage mean?)*. Some questions will invite you to consider how God's Word challenges or supports you in your relationships with God and others *(What does the passage mean to me?)*. Finally, the questions will lead you to examine your actions in light of Scripture *(What am I going to do about it?)*.

Write your responses in this study guide or in a notebook to help you clarify and organize your thoughts and feelings.

THE WEEKLY SMALL-GROUP MEETING

The weekly small-group sharing is the heart of the Little Rock Scripture Study Program. Participants gather in small groups to share the results of praying, reading, and reflecting on Scripture and on the assigned questions. The goal of the discussion is for group members to be strengthened and nourished individually and as a community through sharing how God's Word speaks to them and affects their daily lives. The daily study questions will guide the discussion; it is not necessary to discuss all the questions.

All members share the responsibility of creating an atmosphere of loving support and trust in the group by respecting the opinions and experiences of others, and by affirming and encouraging one another. The simple shared prayer which begins and ends each small group meeting also helps create the open and trusting environment in which group members can share their faith deeply and grow in the study of God's Word.

A distinctive feature of this program is its emphasis on and trust in God's presence working in and through each member. Sharing responses to God's presence in the Word and in others can bring about remarkable growth and transformation.

THE WRAP-UP LECTURE

The lecture is designed to develop and clarify the themes of the lesson. It is not intended to form the basis for the group discussion. For this reason the lecture is always held at the end of the meeting. If several small groups meet at one time, the large group will gather together in a central location to listen to the lecture.

Lectures may be given by a local speaker. They are also available on audio- or video-cassette.

LESSON 1 2 Corinthians 1–2
CBC-NT volume 7, pages 5–9, 83–94

Day 1
1. What is most appealing to you about St. Paul's life or teaching?
2. What did you learn about Paul's relationship to the Corinthians from reading the commentary and the introduction in your Bible?
3. Why do some scholars believe 2 Corinthians is a compilation of several letters?

Day 2
4. a) In what practical ways can the Christian life be a "ministry of encouragement" (1:3-7)? (See Acts 11:22-23; Rom 15:4; Heb 3:13.)
   b) Do you know someone who is especially gifted in this ministry?
5. How has Paul's experience of affliction brought him new freedom (1:8-9)? (See Heb 2:14-15.)
6. Has the danger of death made any impact in your life?

Day 3
7. a) In what ways have you been helped by the prayers of others (1:11)? (See Rom 15:30-32; Col 4:3-4.)
   b) For whom do you pray most often?
8. How will the Corinthians be Paul's boast on the last day (1:14)? (See Phil 2:16; 1 Thess 2:19-20.)
9. A Christian's life is a yes to God (1:17-20). (See Luke 1:38.) What are the main challenges to faithful discipleship today?

Day 4

10. How does Paul express love by causing pain to the Corinthians (2:3-4)? (See Prov 13:24; Heb 12:11.)
11. Have the demands of love ever required you to cause pain and misunderstanding? How did you feel?
12. What is a good way to call an offender in the Church community to correction (2:5-8)? (See Matt 18:15-16.)

Day 5

13. What are some methods for correction that might cause further harm to the individual and the community.
14. How is forgiveness a weapon against Satan (2:10-11)?
15. What role did Titus play in Paul's ministry (2:13)? (See 2 Cor 8:23; 12:18; Gal 2:1; Titus 1:4.)

Day 6

16. How can a Christian be the "aroma of Christ" in the world (2:15)? (See Matt 5:13-16; 1 Cor 5:8.)
17. Comment on the saying: "God doesn't call the qualified, he qualifies the called" (2:16-17). (See John 15:16; 2 Cor 3:5.)

LESSON 2 2 Corinthians 3–4
CBC-NT volume 7, pages 94–99

Day 1

1. What is one lesson you recall from last week's discussion or lecture?
2. How are the Corinthians Paul's letter of recommendation (3:2-3)?
3. Your life is a letter written by God to the world. What message do you hope it is conveying?

Day 2

4. What role do you serve in the ministry of the new covenant (3:5-6)?
5. Paul makes a negative contrast between the old covenant and the new (3:7-8). What was his attitude toward the Jewish religion? (See Rom 9:4-5.)
6. What does Paul mean by contrasting the "ministry of condemnation" and the "ministry of righteousness" (3:9)?

Day 3

7. Paul speaks of the veil over Moses' face and the veil which remained to cloud the people's thoughts (3:13-14). What veils our ability to see God clearly?
8. How can you tell when a person has been transformed by Christ (3:18)? (See Luke 6:43-45; 7:47; Gal 5:22.)
9. In the process of your own growth and transformation, what or who helps you the most?

Day 4

10. What kinds of experiences do you think would discourage a Christian minister (4:1)? (See Mark 8:17-21.)
11. What is your reaction when a member of the clergy proves unfaithful or untruthful (4:2)? (See 1 Thess 2:3.)
12. How is a Christian a bearer of treasures (4:7)?

Day 5

13. a) Do you know someone who is joyful in spite of suffering (4:10)?
    b) Have you had an experience when suffering led to deeper peace and joy?
14. How should our hope of bodily resurrection affect our living now (4:11)? (See 1 Cor 6:13-20.)
15. a) What is the appropriate response to an outpounng of grace (4:15)?
    b) What are some reasons people fail to recognize God's action in their lives?

Day 6

16. In what parts of the world have we seen inner renewal in spite of great material suffering (4:16)?
17. Name two things that make it difficult for people to see deeper realities (4:18).

LESSON 3   2 Corinthians 5–7
CBC-NT volume 7, pages 99–106

Day 1
1. a) What is one theme that surfaced in last week's discussion or lecture?
   b) Is this a concern in your life at this time?
2. Why does Paul speak of our present condition as "living in a tent" (5:1-2)? (See Num 9:22; 1 Cor 15:53; Heb 13:14.)
3. If the Spirit is the "first installment" (5:5), what will the completion bring? (See 1:22; Eph 1:14.)

Day 2
4. What does it mean to "walk by faith, not by sight" (5:7)?
5. Does the prospect of dying frighten you (5:8)? (See Phil 1:23-24; Heb 2:14-15.)
6. a) What are some signs of living for Christ rather than living for oneself (5:14-15)?
   b) Give an example of someone acting fearlessly for Christ without fear of death.

Day 3
7. What are some practical ways we can each be ministers of reconciliation (5:18)? (See Rom 5:10-11.)
8. What are some of the hardships of Christian ministry faced today (6:4-10)?
9. a) Why does Paul endure so much for the gospel (6:1-10)? (See Phil 3:8-11.)
   b) Does Paul's endurance have an impact on your faith?

Day 4

10. What do you believe is the appropriate Christian response to mistreatment (6:8)? (See Exod 5:21; Jer 38:4.)

11. Do you give yourself reminders that you are the "temple of the living God" (6:16)? Give examples. (See Gen 28:15; Eph 3:17-19; Col 1:27.)

12. Relate Paul's anxiety over the Corinthians to that of a parent with children (7:24). (See 1 Thess 2:11-12.)

Day 5

13. How did the arrival of Titus encourage Paul (7:6-7)? (See 1:3-4.)

14. Why is Paul glad that the Corinthians were saddened by his letter (7:8-9)?

15. What examples could you use to illustrate the truth of 7:10? (See Jas 1:2-3; 1 Pet 1:6-7.)

Day 6

16. When is it best not to defend oneself, even when falsely accused (7:11)? (See Isa 53:7; Matt 26:62-63; Acts 26:24-29.)

17. How has Paul's "boasting" before Titus proved true (7:14)?

18. How was Titus' perception of the Corinthians transformed (7:15)? (See 2:9.)

LESSON 4   2 Corinthians 8–9
CBC-NT volume 7, pages 106–110

Day 1
1. What is one lesson you learned about ministry from the discussions or lectures in the last two weeks?
2. What was the good example of the Macedonians that Paul hopes the Corinthians will imitate (8:1-4)?
3. How did their donation express a deeper gift (8:5)? (See Acts 4:34-35.)

Day 2
4. What are the blessings of tithing (8:11-12)? (See Mal 3:10.)
5. How do you determine your contribution to the Church (in terms of time, talents, and possessions)?
6. What do you believe are the most worthy fund appeals?

Day 3
7. How is Jesus a model of charity (8:9)? (See Rom 5:7-8.)
8. When is it hardest to give (8:11-12)? (See Luke 21:1-4.)
9. Why does Paul make special mention of the good qualities of Titus and his unnamed companions (8:16-23)?

Day 4

10. Why does Paul take precautions against handling the money himself (8:20)?

11. How are money decisions handled in your parish?

12. Should you think of yourself as a "holy one" or "saint" (9:1)? Explain. (See 1 Cor 16:1; Eph 1:1.)

Day 5

13. Does Paul mean by the axiom in 9:6 that those who give generously will become wealthy? Explain.

14. How does "God loves a cheerful giver" (9:7) apply to things other than money?

15. How does the collection produce thanksgiving to God (9:11-12)?

Day 6

16. a) How are the anonymous poor and drifters cared for in your town or parish? (See Matt 25:37-40.)
    b) In what ways can you contribute to a ministry of this kind?

17. Was there a time in your life when someone came to your financial rescue? How did you feel?

LESSON 5   2 Corinthians 10–11
CBC-NT volume 7, pages 110–116

Day 1

1. What is one insight you gained from last week's discussion of generous giving?
2. Give an example of Christ's "gentleness and clemency" from the Gospels (10:1).
3. a) Have you ever received gentleness when you expected harshness? How did it affect you? (See 1 Thess 1:7.)
   b) Have you been gentle when harshness was expected?

Day 2

4. a) What does our society consider as powerful weapons in today's world?
   b) In contrast, what do you learn about power from 10:3-5?
5. Why is Paul so insistent on his authority and strength (10:10-11)?
6. When is boasting legitimate (10:13-17)? (See 1 Cor 1:28-29.)

Day 3

7. Who is the virgin Paul speaks of in 11:2? (See Eph 5:25-27; Rev 14:4.)
8. How is marriage a reflection of God's covenant (11:2)? (See Hos 2:21-22; Mal 2:10-16.)
9. What does Paul mean by "superapostles" (11:5)? (See 12:11.)

Day 4

10. Paul is criticized for his lack of speaking ability (11:6). What kind of preaching appeals to you? (See 2 Tim 4:2.)

11. Why didn't Paul accept financial support from the Corinthians (11:7-9)? (See 1 Cor 9:12-18.)

12. What do you learn from Paul's attitude toward accepting their money?

Day 5

13. How can religion be used against people (11:20)? (See Gal 2:4.)

14. What is the purpose of Paul's boasting in 11:22-23?

15. Why do you suppose that Paul's suffering did not cause him to abandon the gospel (11:24-27)?

Day 6

16. What kind of anxiety might a pastor have for a pansh today (11:28)? (See Acts 20:28; Gal 4:19.)

17. What kind of family experiences might make one feel weak and in need of God's help (11:29-30)?

18. Why boast of weakness (11:30)? (See 2 Cor 12:10.)

LESSON 6 2 Corinthians 12–13
CBC-NT volume 7, pages 116–120

Day 1

1. What is the most important lesson you have learned about Paul's relationship to the Corinthians?
2. Why does Paul speak of his prayer experience in a roundabout way (12:2-4)?
3. What are some ways you could prepare for personal prayer time that is fruitful?

Day 2

4. a) Are you able to recognize and acknowledge the special gifts the Lord has given you (12:6)? (See 1 Cor 7:7; 12:4-6.)
   b) Mention one gift you have recognized in the person to your right in the discussion group.
5. For a personal reflection: What is a "thorn in the flesh" in your life (12:7)? Ask Jesus for the grace to carry this cross with him.
6. Have you ever seen good come from humiliation (12:10)? (See Sir 2:4-5; Jas 4:6.)

Day 3

7. Comment on the statement that "when I am weak, then I am strong" (12:10).
8. Paul felt foolish (12:11) and could have erased what he had written. Why do you think he let it stand?
9. Are there instances today when a child might say "I want not what is yours, but you" (12:14)? (See 1 Thess 2:8.)

Day 4

10. Why do people like to spread negative information about others (12:16)? (See Prov 26:22; Sir 19:9-11.)

11. a) How can you defend yourself against slander (12:16-17)?
    b) Have you ever seen slander proved wrong?

12. Why does Paul think his third visit may be painful (12:20)?

Day 5

13. How does the realization that "Jesus Christ is in you" affect your life (13:5)? (Eph 3:20-21; Col 1:27.)

14. Do you know someone who has undergone suffering or loss because of dedication to honesty (13:8)? (See Matt 5:10.)

15. Over the past five years, what is the most significant improvement in your everyday Christian living (13:9)?

Day 6

16. Which of Paul's admonitions in 13:11 might be the most difficult to observe?

17. The closing verse (13:13) may be familiar to you. If so, why?

18. What have you learned about St. Paul from this letter?

NOTES